Timeless Originals

Timeless Originals

A 90-Day Devotional
Using God's Original
Design for Parenting!

parenting
by Design

W. WinePressPublishing
Great Books, Defined.

© 2011 by Parenting By Design, Inc. (Chris Groff). All rights reserved.

WinePress Publishing (PO Box 428, Enumclaw, WA 98022) functions only as book publisher. As such, the ultimate design, content, editorial accuracy, and views expressed or implied in this work are those of the author.

No part of this publication may be reproduced, stored in a retrieval system, or transmitted in any form or by any means—electronic, mechanical, photocopying, recording, or otherwise—without prior written permission from Parenting by Design.

All Scripture quotations, unless otherwise indicated, are taken from the *New American Standard Bible*, © 1960, 1963, 1968, 1971, 1972, 1973, 1975, 1977, 1995 by The Lockman Foundation. Used by permission.

Scripture quotations marked NET are taken from *The NET Bible*® Copyright © 2005 by Biblical Studies Press, L.L.C. www.bible.org. All Rights Reserved. Scripture quoted by permission.

Scripture quotations marked NIV are taken from the *Holy Bible, New International Version*®, *NIV*®. Copyright © 1973, 1978, 1984 by Biblica, Inc.™ Used by permission of Zondervan. All rights reserved worldwide. www.zondervan.com

Scripture quotations marked NLT are taken from the *Holy Bible, New Living Translation*, copyright © 1996, 2004 by Tyndale Charitable Trust. Used by permission of Tyndale House Publishers, Wheaton, Illinois 60189. All rights reserved.

Scripture quotations marked NKJV are taken from the *New King James Version*, © 1979, 1980, 1982 by Thomas Nelson, Inc., Publishers. Used by permission.

ISBN 13: 978-1-60615-070-2
ISBN 10: 1-60615-070-7
Library of Congress Catalog Card Number: 2010933050

Contents

Introduction vii

Week One 1
Week Two 9
Week Three 17
Week Four 25
Week Five 33
Week Six 41
Week Seven 49
Week Eight 57
Week Nine 65
Week Ten 73
Week Eleven 81
Week Twelve 89
Week Thirteen 97

About the Authors 107

Introduction

As we sat at a residential drug treatment center in 2003 with our youngest son, Chris and I realized we needed help to deal with the parenting issues we were facing. But never in a million years did we anticipate how God would use this parenting struggle to change the direction of our lives and call us back to Him.

With the help of our son's therapist, Lee Long, we began to discover God's timeless and original parenting principles—principles that have helped restore our family and vastly improve our relationships with our two sons.

Along with Lee's wife, Charlotte, Chris and I wrote this book of devotionals to reflect these principles, and we hope it will be a source of inspiration for you to draw from daily. Each devotion is written with parents like you in mind—parents who are passionate about their children but who want real, biblical answers to the questions they face every day.

Timeless Originals has been developed with an understanding that when you're holding in your arms something as precious—and original—as your child, you want to invest in proven and lasting principles you can trust.

Timeless Originals

So whether you're a new parent or an empty-nester, our prayer is that *Timeless Originals* will draw you closer to our heavenly Father and equip and encourage you to lovingly guide your family with His original parenting design.

—Michelle Groff

Week One

Day 1: Discipline and Love

For whom the Lord loves He reproves, even as a father corrects the son in whom he delights (Prov. 3:12).

As hard as it is to deliver a consequence to a child for a bad choice, the alternative can often be even worse. When I am tempted to forego discipline, I have to ask myself, *What is the most loving thing I can do for my child?* In almost every case, the answer is to give the child the consequence he has earned so he can learn the lesson God has designed for him.

A good consequence, delivered with empathy, demonstrates love and respect for your child's freedom to choose and his or her ability to learn from the consequence of a bad decision. The author of Hebrews says it well: "All discipline for the moment seems not to be joyful, but sorrowful; yet to those who have been trained by it, afterwards it yields the peaceful fruit of righteousness" (Heb. 12:11).

Delivering consistent consequences with empathy is an act of love.

Day 2: Empathy

Speaking the truth in love, we are to grow up in all aspects into Him who is the head, even Christ (Eph. 4:15).

John Stott once said, "Our love grows soft if it is not strengthened by truth, and our truth grows hard if it is not softened by love." The essence of empathy is balancing truth and love. A rescuing parent leans heavily on love but shies away from truth. A dictating parent leans heavily on truth but mixes in little love. A counselor parent is able to express love no matter what the child says or does, yet is strong enough to deliver appropriate consequences and to allow his or her child to struggle so that *real* learning takes place.

Our anxiety or anger will often reveal where we fall on the continuum between rescuer and dictator. Is your love too soft, or your truth too hard? Striking a balance between truth and love models our heavenly Father's relationship with us.

Day 3: Hope in the Unseen

For in hope we have been saved, but hope that is seen is not hope; for who hopes for what he already sees? But if we hope for what we do not see, with perseverance we wait eagerly for it (Rom. 8:24–25).

As Christians, we know how the story of our lives is going to end, yet the hope into which we have been saved is unseen. What we *can* see is the world and its demands. Unless we keep our minds focused on the unseen, the pressure to live for today's culture will swallow us up. The ever-present media (TV, magazines, newspapers, Internet) distracts us from God's truth and lures us with the false hope of instant gratification. Fortunately, God provides a defense: "The Spirit of Him who raised Jesus from the dead dwells in you" (Rom. 8:11).

Week One

Demonstrate an eternal perspective for your kids. Talk about the messages the culture is sending to them and contrast those messages with the hope that we have as followers of Christ.

Day 4: Trusting God (Part I)

Look among the nations! Observe! Be astonished! Wonder! Because I am doing something in your days—you would not believe if you were told (Hab. 1:5).

Taken out of context, this verse sounds encouraging. The reality of the situation, however, was that God was telling Habakkuk that He was about to unleash the evil Babylonians on the nation of Judah. The Jews were about to be overrun, killed, and taken into captivity, and the Temple in Jerusalem was about to be destroyed as punishment for Israel's years of disobedience.

God does many amazing works using means we cannot even imagine. In parenting, God will work through the trials that you and your children face in ways that will astonish you—ways that "you would not believe if you were told." This should be a great comfort to you when your kids make really bad choices and the consequences seem harsh or unbearable.

As the apostle Paul said, "Oh, the depth of the riches both of the wisdom and knowledge of God! How unsearchable are his judgments and how unfathomable His ways! ... For from Him and through Him and to Him are all things. To Him be glory forever" (Rom. 11:33,36).

Day 5: Trusting God (Part II)

Though the fig tree may not blossom, nor fruit be on the vines; though the labor of the olive may fail, and the fields yield no food; though the flock may be cut off from the fold, and there be no herd in the stall—yet I will rejoice in the Lord, I will joy in the God of my salvation (Hab. 3:17–18, NKJV).

Are you concerned that your children may be headed down a path they should not follow? God tells us that when this occurs, we must trust Him. He has a plan for our children's lives. Habakkuk had to face the truth that his nation was about to be destroyed for its disobedience, but he found a way to trust and even rejoice in the Lord, knowing that God's ways were impossible to fully understand. He knew God was working, and that his job was to wait quietly and let God's will be done.

The psalmist described this level of trust in Psalm 46:10: "Be still, and know that I am God; I will be exalted among the nations; I will be exalted in the earth!" (NKJV).

Trust God. His plan is perfect, even when it seems so contrary to our own.

Weekend Reflection: Days 6 and 7

by Michelle Groff

> **How Original**
> Before basketball games at my son's Catholic elementary school, it is customary for the players, coaches and referees to recite the "Our Father." One time, as they gathered on the court in a circle and held hands, my daughter exclaimed, "Are they going to do the hokey pokey?"
> —Sami M., age 4

Don't you love seeing life through the eyes of children? They come up with some of the most entertaining and unique descriptions of the world around them. Until they develop the ability to think abstractly, they interpret life in *very* literal terms. Simply put, their perspective is limited.

Stories like this remind me that as a child of God, I also have a limited perspective. This becomes particularly apparent to me in desperate moments when I am forced to confront the limits of my human understanding.

I remember when my youngest son relapsed in his struggle against drug addiction. I found myself doubting God's wisdom. "Why, Lord, why?" I asked. To say that I was overcome with fear would be an understatement. But moments like this often yield the most clarity. For me, that meant asking myself one question: *Do you believe God is good?*

As I reflected on God's faithful hand in my life, I knew in my heart the answer was yes. I also knew that my challenge was to trust in His goodness regardless of my present circumstances. This meant embracing the reality of my limited and childlike perspective. It meant accepting that my "hokey pokey" was His "Our Father."

My son's journey led to an eighteen-month stay at a residential treatment program. During his time there, he started reading the Bible and dedicated his life to the Lord. When he left the program, he got a job and enrolled in a Bible college. His goal today is to become a pastor.

I am almost hesitant to share the outcome of our situation, because the reality is God doesn't always give us the happy ending we crave. God would have been no less good if the story had played out differently. Here is where we can learn from our children's example: We must realize there is a bigger perspective that is, for the moment, beyond our grasp. Like our kids, "We see but a poor reflection as in a mirror; then we shall see face to face. Now I know in part, but then I will know fully just as I also have been fully known" (1 Cor. 13:12).

In the meantime, we can have faith in the words of the psalmist: "Give thanks to the Lord, for he is good; his love endures forever" (Ps. 106:1, NIV).

Notes

Week Two

Day 8: Power from the Word of God

For whatever was written in earlier times was written for our instruction, so that through perseverance and the encouragement of the Scriptures we might have hope (Rom. 15:4).

In this verse, Paul highlights one of the sources of the spiritual power we need: the Word of God. Tapping into this power enables us to be the kind of parents God designed us to be. We can try so hard to be empathetic or understanding and yet find ourselves frustrated and discouraged. That is when we need to spend some quiet time with God and His Book, praying and seeking the direction that only He can provide.

Bible study has many values, but this verse promises that the Scriptures will encourage us. Haven't you found that to be true in your life? Studying the Bible through the lens of parenting can sustain you through those trying parenting moments.

Disciplined Bible study will prepare you for the parenting challenges ahead. Stay prepared!

Timeless Originals

Day 9: Just Say No

Yet the news about him spread all the more, so that crowds of people came to hear him and to be healed of their sicknesses. But Jesus often withdrew to lonely places and prayed (Luke 5:15–16, NIV).

Parenting puts tremendous demands on our time and energy. Those demands can start before our kids get up in the morning and last long after they have fallen asleep. In addition, we often find ourselves meeting the needs of others in our family, satisfying the demands of people at work, and rushing to help our friends.

Jesus knows the extent of our weariness. Many people besieged Him when they discovered He could heal the sick and perform miracles. There was no end to the ingenious ways they devised just to touch Him or get His attention (see Luke 5:18–19). Jesus recognized this huge demand for His time, but He also knew that the only way He could deal with it was to spend time alone with His Father to rest, pray, and recharge His batteries. This wasn't selfish; it was the most loving thing He could do for His children. It gave Him the energy and strength He needed to deal with their many issues.

Sometimes, saying no to your kids so you can spend quality time with your heavenly Father is the most loving thing you can do for them.

Week Two

Day 10: Surrender

I planted, Apollos watered, but God was causing the growth. So then neither the one who plants nor the one who waters is anything, but God who causes the growth (1 Cor. 3:6–7).

We can put a lot of pressure on ourselves to produce "successful" kids, and there is no question that parenting requires a lot of hard work. But what exactly is our role in the process? In this passage Paul explains the role of a teacher, and it applies just as well to a parent.

Parents are God's representatives in the family, and that role is crucially important. In the end, however, we have to surrender the results to God, because He is the One "who causes the growth." He will grow our children into His design. While it is difficult to let go of our plans and surrender our kids to God, it is God's will that they grow less dependent on us and more dependent on Him.

You cannot force your children to grow up to be godly, but you can be a godly parent. Use your children's experiences, your example and gentle exploration to "plant and water" your kids—and then surrender the results to God.

Day 11: Living as an Alien

Dear friends, I urge you, as aliens and strangers in the world, to abstain from sinful desires, which war against your soul. Live such good lives among the pagans that, though they accuse you of doing wrong, they may see your good deeds and glorify God on the day he visits us (1 Pet. 2:11–12, NIV).

When many of us travel, we go to great lengths to avoid being labeled as "tourists," but it usually doesn't take long before someone asks us where we're from. The way we talk, dress, and act are clues that identify us with our home.

This passage reminds us that, as Christians, our citizenship is not of this world. Christ calls us to act in a way that reflects our heavenly citizenship, but sometimes we blend in with the culture so well that no one would dream of calling us tourists.

As Christians, our customs and values should be remarkably different from the world. They should be reflected in our words and actions and displayed in our parenting. Sometimes we will feel like aliens. Eyebrows may be raised when we say no to allowing our children to go to inappropriate movies or wear provocative clothes. But maybe someone will be intrigued by our family's "unusual" customs and values.

Shouldn't your family's lifestyle reflect your heavenly citizenship?

Day 12: Gifts and Strengths

But to each one is given the manifestation of the Spirit for the common good. ... But now God has placed the members, each one of them, in the body, just as He desired. If they were all one member, where would the body be? (1 Cor. 12:7,18–19).

God designed each of us for a particular purpose, and He specifically gifted us to accomplish that purpose "for the common good." Yet we often want to design our own purpose for our children and ourselves. Unfortunately, that choice typically includes taking on qualities and characteristics that are honored and esteemed by the world's system. That's not the way God works. God is the architect, and He knows how the pieces fit together.

Don't you think it would be more rewarding to submit to God's design and walk in His will than to struggle to be something you were not designed to be? As Paul states, "All are not apostles, are they?" (1 Cor. 12:29).

Try a spiritual gifts inventory with your family, look for each member's unique design and gifting, and then work together on ways to use those gifts "for the common good."

Timeless Originals

Weekend Reflection: Days 13 and 14

by Michelle Groff

> **How Original**
> My daughter sat at the dinner table and glanced down at the plate of food in front of her. She then stated seriously, "Mom, this is not your best work. I *know* you can do better than this."
>
> —Petra C., age 5

Watching our kids achieve success feels pretty good, doesn't it? There's something about being the parent of the kid who hits the home run, makes the top grade, or becomes head cheerleader that seems to affirm our value as parents. And our culture applauds. But if we're not careful, we can become preoccupied with results and miss the value of the journey.

This was particularly true for Chris and me. We love competition. Trust me, you don't want to play us in Monopoly. Or checkers. Or Go Fish. Or tiddlywinks. We'll make a game out of almost anything in order to "win." Imagine being the innocent child born into this environment! Indeed, it started early. I remember feeling proud that our son scored a 9 on the Apgar scale that rates a newborn's health.

Then I began comparing developmental milestones with other kids his age. I felt a subtle competition for him to be the first to roll over, sit, crawl, stand up, or walk.

When we signed our son up for T-ball, someone should have done an intervention. We coached our four-year-old with all the dedication and scrutiny of a major league manager. We had enjoyed the sweet aroma of success in our own lives, and now we craved it for our son—not to mention the reflected glory it would bring to us as his parents.

"Do your best. Give it your best effort. Give 110 percent." These were our slogans for our son. But how often do any of us do our best all the time? Is that even possible? It sounds like a tremendous amount of pressure, and it's certainly not the standard I want others to apply when scrutinizing my efforts.

It's important to remember that as children of God, our worth is never dependent on our performance. If it were, all of us would be in big trouble. God allows the struggle of disappointments and trials because He knows they encourage us to grow and mature. Instead of success, His focus is walking alongside us as we experience day-to-day life.

Luckily, God doesn't need us to make Him look good. He can do that all on His own.

Notes

Week Three

Day 15: Weakness Versus Strength

But God has chosen the foolish things of the world to shame the wise, and God has chosen the weak things of the world to shame the things which are strong. ... Because the foolishness of God is wiser than men, and the weakness of God is stronger than men (1 Cor. 1:27,25).

The world's definition of "strength" is much different from God's. For example, our culture defines strength as having one or more of the attributes it values the most: money, power, beauty, and fame. Images from the media deluge our children with the idea that a successful person is someone who possesses these qualities.

Yet Christ valued none of these attributes. He came to serve, rather than be served, and to give His life for us. The Corinthians did not understand *that* kind of strength. I wonder whether we are much different.

Reading the Sermon on the Mount (see Matt. 5–7) reminds us who the strong really are—those who do not rely on their own strength but instead rely on God to supply the power.

Teach your children God's concept of a strong person—one who surrenders to God.

Day 16: Balancing Goodness (love) and Severity (truth)

Consider therefore the kindness and sternness of God: sternness to those who fell, but kindness to you, provided that you continue in his kindness (Rom. 11:22, NIV).

It is interesting to note the number of times the Bible describes God as exhibiting two attributes that are opposites. In this verse, those attributes are kindness and sternness. God's love is expressed in His kindness, but it is not His only characteristic. He is also stern with those who disobey Him. He balances these attributes perfectly as He relates to His children.

We are called to imitate God in our relationships with our kids. We cannot always be "kind," because there will be times in their lives when they will rebel and disobey us. We cannot always be "stern," because that will create resentment and fear. A balance between the two is our goal, and God promises to give us the wisdom to achieve that balance (see James 1:5).

Ask God for the wisdom to balance kindness and sternness in your relationships with your children.

Day 17: Help with Prayer

In the same way, the Spirit helps us in our weakness. We do not know what we ought to pray for, but the Spirit himself intercedes for us with groans that words cannot express. And he who searches our hearts knows the mind of the Spirit, because the Spirit intercedes for the saints in accordance with God's will (Rom. 8:26–27, NIV).

Do you ever have trouble praying? Most of us do. This passage tells us that God is fully aware of our weakness in this respect.

Week Three

The good news is that the Spirit is always working to make our deepest needs known to the Father.

The Spirit uses "groans that words cannot express" to present these needs to God. Like a married couple that can finish each other's sentences, God knows exactly what the Spirit is requesting on our behalf. What a relief to know that the Spirit of God is supplementing our feeble prayers!

So if you have trouble with prayer, take heart. The Spirit that raised Jesus from the dead is praying for you.

Day 18: Active Dependence

And he said, "Blessed be the Lord God of my master Abraham, who has not forsaken His mercy and His truth toward my master. As for me, being on the way, the Lord led me to the house of my master's brethren" (Gen. 24:27, NKJV).

When it was time for Isaac to marry, Abraham sent a servant to find a wife from among Abraham's relatives. The servant left for Ur, trusting God to make the choice clear when the time was right. He accomplished his task when he met Rebekah at the well. Notice the servant's response: "As for me, *being on the way, the Lord led me* to the house of my master's brethren" (emphasis added). What a wonderful example of active dependence! The servant embarked on the journey, but he depended on God to guide him to the right woman.

In parenting, "being on the way" means accepting our responsibility to make decisions that affect our kids. Our fear of mistakes may tempt us to avoid decisions, but parenting requires us to act. Thankfully, God does not ask us to rely on our own wisdom. When we acknowledge our dependence on Him and seek His guidance and strength, He promises to provide them to us.

Timeless Originals

Be humble enough to seek God's will, yet bold enough to keep moving forward.

Day 19: Consequences

For this reason a man will leave his father and mother and be united to his wife, and they will become one flesh (Gen. 2:24, NIV).

God's plan for our kids is for them to become progressively less and less dependent on us and eventually leave our home. We can help them develop the skills they are going to need as adults by allowing them to make age-appropriate choices *and* experience the consequences of those choices.

Learning to be a good decision-maker is a skill that is learned, and kids will make mistakes along the way. You will be tempted to intervene to prevent mistakes or rescue your kids from consequences, because you will hate to see them in pain. However, you need to challenge yourself to adopt a long-range perspective. Ask yourself what will be more painful: allowing them to make mistakes while they are under your roof or postponing the learning opportunity until later in life when the stakes are much higher?

When you allow your kids to experience the consequences of their own mistakes, you prepare them to be capable adults.

Week Three

Weekend Reflection: Days 20 and 21

by Michelle Groff

> **How Original**
> One morning my children awoke to find it had snowed. I asked my nine-year-old son to put the dogs outside. After playing for a few minutes, the dogs went about their business. Watching the dogs, our daughter yelled, "Christian, THAT is why you don't eat yellow snow!"
> —Megan C., age 5

"Don't eat yellow snow." Another valuable childhood lesson! My guess is that Megan's mother could have cautioned her all day long about the dangers of *eating* yellow snow, but the lesson wouldn't have been driven home until Megan actually had the experience of seeing her dog *make* yellow snow. So often as parents, we try to accomplish with words what is better taught by observation, experience and consequences.

I know this was true for me. Morning after morning the events around our house unfolded like a movie script. It began with my cheerful attempts to wake my boys up for school. My efforts were usually acknowledged with a grunt as I headed to the kitchen to make breakfast. At some point, it would dawn on me that I had heard no signs of movement. Dutifully, I would return to their rooms, only to find them still deep in their REM cycles.

Next, I would switch to my nagging mode. "C'mon, guys. If you don't get up now, you're going to be late. You're old enough to wake up without my help. Now GET UP!" Certain that nagging would be effective, I would return to the kitchen to finish breakfast. A few minutes would pass, and then I would yell to see if they wanted milk or orange juice.

Timeless Originals

No response. So I would march back to their rooms, only to discover a total lack of progress.

That meant it was time to launch the next weapon in my arsenal: threats. "I can't believe you guys are just ignoring me. If you don't get up right this minute, I'm not going to let you to play on the computer when you get home. I mean it." (By the way, whenever you have to add, "I mean it," it usually means you don't.)

If the definition of insanity is doing the same thing over and over again but expecting a different result, then I was certifiable. At the time, I didn't see any other options. If I let them sleep, they would skip breakfast, making it harder for them to concentrate at school. What self-respecting mother would let her children go to school hungry? And if they were late, they might miss a test or get graded down on an assignment. They might even have to stay for detention on Saturday.

I rationalized that it was my job to prevent these kinds of consequences. Then one day, it dawned on me that I had been willing to allow consequences that were far worse. I had become a human cattle prod. It was an approach that had not won their respect or cooperation. Besides preventing the consequences from teaching them valuable lessons, my methods of communicating were causing our relationship to suffer.

Sometimes words are a poor motivator for lasting change. It usually takes a meaningful experience for a child to make the connection between their actions and a negative consequence.

I'm sure it's why you won't see Megan eating yellow snow.

Notes

Week Four

Day 22: God's Eternal Plan

You intended to harm me, but God intended it for good to accomplish what is now being done, the saving of many lives (Gen. 50:20, NIV).

Joseph endured the evil intentions of many people—his brothers selling him into slavery, Potiphar's wife falsely accusing him, the cupbearer forgetting him, and seven years of famine. Yet God was able to use all of those events to bring about the deliverance of Israel. Through all the disappointments (and the victories), Joseph remained confident that God was in control.

The Bible encourages us to adopt this perspective with our children. They are certain to experience trials and disappointments in their lives—injuries, sickness, rejection by friends, failed tests, dropped balls. At times we may wonder if God truly has a plan. Joseph's story reminds us that God is bigger than our circumstances. Although we may not be able to grasp His overall plan now, one day we will be able to see the beautiful tapestry that has been woven out of the events of our lives and the lives of our children.

"And we know that in *all* things God works for the good of those who love him" (Rom. 8:28, NIV, emphasis added). Look past trials and anticipate God's gracious response.

Timeless Originals

Day 23: Power from the Holy Spirit

Now we have received, not the spirit of the world, but the Spirit who is from God, so that we may know the things freely given to us by God, which things we also speak, not in words taught by human wisdom, but in those taught by the Spirit, combining spiritual thoughts with spiritual words (1 Cor. 2:12–13).

Parenting is a tough job, but fortunately we have the ultimate Helper to guide us. When we became believers, we were filled with the source of parenting wisdom: the Holy Spirit. When confronted with difficult decisions about choices, consequences or showing empathy, a mature Christian knows that turning to "the Spirit who is from God" rather than "the spirit of the world" yields the kind of response that would be impossible under his or her own power. When we turn to the Holy Spirit before we turn to our children, we can speak with the wisdom of God rather than mere "human wisdom."

There are no parenting guides more valuable than the Holy Spirit and prayer.

Day 24: Confession and Repentance

Noah … became drunk and lay uncovered in his tent. Ham, the father of Canaan, saw his father's nakedness and told his two brothers outside (Gen. 9:20–22, NIV).

During the flood, Noah demonstrated obedience to God under incredibly difficult circumstances. His obedience waned, however, when the earth dried. In this particular case, Noah made wine, got drunk, and passed out. His son, Ham, discovered Noah in this dishonorable position and mocked him in front of his brothers. When Noah woke up, he cursed

Ham. It's interesting to note that while Ham was wrong and deserved consequences, Noah wasn't innocent in this situation. He was guilty of setting a poor example.

As parents, we need to humbly admit our sin even when it is commingled with the sin of our children. If we fail to take responsibility for our mistakes and instead focus on the mistakes of our children, we provide an example of blaming and excuse-making. Our kids may conclude that the rules do not apply to people in positions of power or authority.

Our willingness to confess and repent provides a powerful example for our kids.

Day 25: Called to Parenting

Moses said to the Lord, "O Lord, I have never been eloquent. ..." The Lord said to him ... "Now go; I will help you speak and will teach you what to say" (Exod. 4:10–12, NIV).

Sometimes we don't understand why God calls us to a certain task or ministry. Other people seem far more qualified to meet the challenge. Yet, over and over again in the Bible, we see that God uses unlikely people to accomplish His goals.

There is no greater calling from God than parenting. When you feel inadequate for the task, realize that you are putting your trust in the wrong person. Strive to be an excellent parent, but recognize that God is not dependent on your knowledge or expertise to bring about His results.

When you feel overwhelmed, surrender control and trust God. He will provide.

Timeless Originals

Day 26: "Seeing" Your Children

She gave this name to the Lord who spoke to her: "You are the God who sees me," for she said, "I have seen the One who sees me" (Gen. 16:13, NIV).

This passage tells of the trials of Hagar, the maid of Sarai. Sarai was unable to conceive, so she sent Hagar to Abram, hoping Hagar would bear a child in her place. When Hagar became pregnant, however, animosity developed between the two women. Sarai's subsequent mistreatment caused Hagar to run away into the desert. There, God intervened and encouraged Hagar. She knew that He truly understood her struggle, and as a result, she felt deeply known by God. She even named God: "You are the God who sees me." This gave her the strength to go back and fulfill her responsibilities to Sarai in the midst of tough circumstances.

Like Hagar, our kids desperately long to be seen and known by their parents. How can we do this? By taking time to discover and celebrate their interests, by appreciating their unique qualities (no matter how different they are from our own), and by listening to their perspective on life.

When we discover and value our kids' God-given uniqueness, they feel known and accepted.

Weekend Reflection: Days 27 and 28

by Michelle Groff

> **How Original**
> My husband, our son Isaac, and I were grocery shopping one night. I was scratching Isaac's back as we walked along, and he said, "That feels so good, if I had a tail, I'd be waggin' it!"
> —Isaac S., age 8

It's true that having our back scratched feels great, but there's something we can do for our kids that feels even better: listen to them. Listening is an art form that few of us have taken the time and energy to perfect. Sure, we've got other "skills" down pat … lecturing, nagging, advising, commanding, begging and arguing. Just put us on a debate team, and we're good to go! But listening requires something deeper. It requires "curiosity." Are you more interested in discovering how your child sees the world or in showing them your point of view? Are you curious to learn about their passions, or would you rather teach them about yours?

When my boys were in their teens, I became convicted that I needed to talk less and listen more. But old habits die hard. Just a few sentences into a conversation, I would find myself offering my opinion or giving advice. Some motherly button inside me was pushed, and the next thing I knew, our conversation had turned into a running critique. Example:

> **Son:** "Mom, the coolest thing happened today! I was running late to science when …"
>
> **Me:** "Why were you running late to science? I sure wish being on time was a priority for you. Does the teacher grade you down for a certain number of tardies?"

Son: "I don't know. Well anyway, it was right after lunch. I was racing to class and stopped to get a Coke from the machine …"

Me: "You were late to class because you were getting a Coke?"

Son: "Um, I don't know. I guess so."

Me: "I really didn't intend for your lunch money to be spent on Cokes. How often do you drink them at school?"

Son: "Hardly at all. Never mind. I gotta go."

Me: "No, wait, I want to hear …"

And I wondered why they didn't open up! My communication skills were causing me to miss out on great opportunities to know my kids.

What a contrast to our heavenly Father. Day in and day out, He calls us into an authentic relationship with Him. He takes the time to listen to us and make us feel deeply known. He unconditionally accepts us despite our shortcomings. He is patient in how He reveals areas in which we need to change. He delights in our unique qualities.

Consider the words of David in Psalm 139:1–4: "O Lord, you have searched me and you know me. You know when I sit and when I rise; You perceive my thoughts from afar. You discern my going out and my lying down; You are familiar with all my ways. Before a word is on my tongue You know it completely, O Lord" (NIV).

How great it is to be "known." Let's follow God's lead and be students of our children's unique personalities. Start by listening to them, and then watch them respond. You just might find your tail wagging, too!

Notes

Week Five

Day 29: Discipline, Character and Hope

But we also exult in our tribulations, knowing that tribulation brings about perseverance; and perseverance, proven character; and proven character, hope; and hope does not disappoint, because the love of God has been poured out within our hearts through the Holy Spirit who was given to us (Rom. 5:3–5).

When our children suffer—whether from their own bad choices or those of someone else—we want so badly to rescue them from the pain or tell them how to avoid finding themselves in that predicament again. But God has another plan: to perfect them through their trials. Character-building lessons are rarely learned from the triumphs of life; rather, it is the trials we endure that teach us how to persevere despite the pain. Taking trials away from our kids deprives them of the chance to grow, build character and learn to hope in God.

The best character-building lessons are learned from trials. Don't inhibit your children's growth by rescuing them or by assuming responsibility for their difficult situations.

Day 30: Detours

When Pharaoh let the people go, God did not lead them on the road through the Philistine country, though that was shorter (Exod. 13:17, NIV).

After God delivered the Israelites from Egypt, He did not lead them on a direct path to the Promised Land. Instead, He opted for a route that avoided certain obstacles and challenged them to evaluate their hearts. In the same way, during the course of our parenting journey, God will sometimes take us on detours that seem counterproductive. While we may have a wonderful story written for the lives of our children, it is usually one that does not include pain and hardship. Inevitably, God's story takes our children to places that we wouldn't choose, but these are the very routes that will help them develop maturity, integrity and perseverance.

When you are in the midst of one of these detours, challenge yourself to adopt God's eternal perspective. He is making your kids more like Him.

Day 31: Be Still

Moses answered the people, "Do not be afraid. Stand firm and you will see the deliverance the Lord will bring you today. The Egyptians you see today you will never see again. The Lord will fight for you; you need only to be still" (Exod. 14:13–14, NIV).

Trapped against the sea, the Israelites watched in terror as the Egyptians appeared in hot pursuit. Moses alone remained calm and encouraged the people not to be afraid. He challenged them to be still and allow the Lord to fight for them.

Week Five

As we raise our children, we will also be faced with panic-inducing situations. If we do not have a solid foundation of faith, we may be overcome with fear and tempted to act rashly. Instead, God asks us to pause and seek His guidance. He reminds us that the battle is His. Obviously, this requires us to depend on His wisdom instead of our own. Sometimes, the hardest thing to do is to be still.

When faced with difficult parenting situations, seek God's guidance *before* you act.

Day 32: Daily Dependence

Then the Lord said to Moses, "I will rain down bread from heaven for you. The people are to go out each day and gather enough for that day. In this way I will test them and see whether they will follow my instructions" (Exod. 16:4, NIV).

We often long for God to reveal the whole path before us, but He usually gives us only one stepping-stone at a time. When the Israelites were wandering in the desert, God set up a system that required them to trust in His provision on a daily basis. He knew self-sufficiency would draw them away from Him.

It can be difficult to choose a path of daily dependence on God for our lives and the lives of our children. We desperately want to plan, orchestrate, and manipulate all the details, because it gives us a sense of control. The illusion of control, however, can tempt us to rely on ourselves instead of God.

Are you holding tightly to your sense of control, or are you depending on God for guidance? Trust your children to God each morning. He knows what He's doing.

Day 33: The Validation of the World

When Rachel saw that she was not bearing Jacob any children, she became jealous of her sister. ... Then she said, "Here is Bilhah, my maidservant. Sleep with her so that she can bear children for me and that through her I too can build a family" (Gen. 30:1–3, NIV).

Ancient Middle Eastern culture placed great value on women who could bear children, especially sons. Jacob's wives, Rachel and Leah, were sisters and rivals who used childbearing (either by giving birth themselves or through their maidservants) to bolster their own sense of self-worth. As they focused on validating themselves by worldly standards, their competition quickly degenerated and produced sinful attitudes and behaviors.

Like Rachel and Leah, we can define our worth, and the worth of our children, by achievements and the ability to possess what others value. However, when we measure our significance in these ways, we become slaves to the thoughts and opinions of the world rather than the thoughts and opinions of God.

Remember where your true citizenship lies. Rest in your identity in Christ instead of chasing after worldly validation.

Week Five

Weekend Reflection: Days 34 and 35

by Michelle Groff

> **How Original**
> When sorting through my daughter's toys to donate to Goodwill, Chloe was upset that she had to give some away, even though she no longer played with them. She asked in a disgruntled voice, "Man, is good Will ever bad? He gets a lot of stuff!"
> —Chloe N., age 5

Do you have any "good Wills" in your life? You know—the people who seem to have everything. If you're not careful, you may be tempted to compare your lifestyles, your achievements and even your kids to others. Nothing will steal your contentment more quickly.

When I am in the middle of a pity party, I think about Kokeh Kotee. Kokeh left Liberia to attend Dallas Theological Seminary. His goal was to become better equipped to minister to Liberian pastors. Upon graduation, he did the unthinkable: He actually returned to Liberia.

Why was this so remarkable? Two brutal civil wars had killed more than 200,000 people and decimated Liberia's infrastructure. The wars had left the country without running water, electricity, or a functioning sewage system. Unemployment was at 85 percent, and crime was rampant. Malnutrition, diarrhea, cholera, and malaria were major health issues. As a result, most professionals had long ago left the country for greener economic pastures.

For Kokeh, any other location, and especially Dallas, would have been a dramatic improvement. Compared to Liberia,

Timeless Originals

Kokeh's quality of life while attending seminary was downright opulent. Working toilets. Air conditioning. Plenty of food. Access to medical care. When graduation rolled around, it would have been easy for him to rationalize maintaining this comfortable lifestyle. It would also have been easy for him to compare his limited economic prospects to those of his fellow graduates. But Kokeh didn't compare Liberia to Dallas or any other city. His sense of success wasn't defined by salary or living conditions, but in obeying God's call for his life.

Our kids face a battlefield every bit as dangerous and toxic as the war-torn streets of Liberia. It's a culture that bombards them with false standards of value—standards in which they are likely to come up woefully short.

Victory from this enemy is found in Jesus. He asks us not to compare our circumstances with "good Will" or anyone else. As parents, we can show our kids that contentment comes from focusing on Christ and obeying His call.

Notes

Week Six

Day 36: Faith Stories

Only be careful, and watch yourselves closely so that you do not forget the things your eyes have seen or let them slip from your heart as long as you live. Teach them to your children and to their children after them (Deut. 4:9, NIV).

It is amazing how quickly we can forget or dismiss the ways God has been faithful to us in the past. We easily become distracted, self-sufficient, or focused on a new problem. God knows these human tendencies, which is why He asks us to actively remember His blessings. In fact, He takes it one step further by instructing us to share these stories with our children. Children learn from example. If parents model a faith that is alive and real, it will have incredible influence on their lives.

In Ephesians 6:16, Paul talks about taking up the shield of faith to defend against the evil one. Your family's shield of faith can be constructed with stories of God's faithfulness and provision.

Take the time to communicate to your kids the many ways God has blessed you. It will be an affirmation for you and an example to them.

Day 37: Discipline is an Example

Be conscientious about how you live and what you teach. Persevere in this, because by doing so you will save both yourself and those who listen to you (1 Tim. 4:16, NET).

Being prepared for godly parenting requires a close, daily walk with God. After all, He is the father of all humankind. He has had billions of children. And He has recorded His thoughts and experiences as an example for our parenting journey. Read the Bible through the lens of parenting and you will be amazed at the wealth of knowledge it contains.

In this passage, Paul told Timothy that he needed to be disciplined in *his* life before he could be effective in the lives of *others*. Later, Paul told him where the ultimate example was found: "All Scripture is God-breathed and is useful for teaching, rebuking, correcting and training in righteousness, so that the man of God may be thoroughly equipped for every good work" (2 Tim. 3:16–17, NIV).

Studying the Bible helps you emulate God and allows His wisdom to shine through you.

Day 38: Power from Prayer

Now may the God who gives perseverance and encouragement grant you to be of the same mind with one another according to Christ Jesus, so that with one accord you may with one voice glorify the God and Father of our Lord Jesus Christ (Rom. 15:5–6).

Parenting is a team sport. When you and your spouse (or friends, if you are a single parent) are "of the same mind with one another according to Christ Jesus," you can make the kind of parenting decisions that will be the best for everyone in the family. These verses are a helpful prayer for parents. With the aid of the Holy Spirit, the result will be appropriate choices, great consequences, and the empathy necessary to deliver both. By praying and seeking God's will together, you and your spouse (or friends) can with "one voice glorify the God and Father of our Lord Jesus Christ."

Each spouse can learn something from the other. Single parents can learn from friends who are parents. When you talk about difficult parenting situations and pray together for guidance, you glorify God.

Day 39: No Guarantees

When Samuel grew old, he appointed his sons as judges for Israel. ... But his sons did not walk in his ways. They turned aside after dishonest gain and accepted bribes and perverted justice (1 Sam. 8:1,3, NIV).

Even if we are the godliest parents in the world, we are not guaranteed godly children. Why? Because children have free will and live in a fallen world, just like us. They have the choice to follow our example and the instruction we give them, or not. As this verse relates, the prophet Samuel walked with God faithfully, yet his children turned out so poorly that the people demanded a king to replace them as judges. God honored Samuel's faithfulness in many ways, but his example was not reflected in the choices of his children.

Parenting is a journey with an uncertain destination. You can't count on a good result just because you are faithful. There is

Timeless Originals

no formula that will assure you that your children will follow Jesus. You must place your trust in God, surrender your children to Him, follow His will the best you can, and leave the results to Him.

You must trust the result of your parenting to God.

Day 40: Focus

Be very strong; be careful to obey all that is written in the Book of the Law of Moses, without turning aside to the right or to the left (Josh. 23:6, NIV).

God has provided guidelines and wisdom to show us how we should live. But our culture opposes these guidelines and sees God's truth as foolishness. Each day, we are bombarded with messages telling us what our children must have or do to "be somebody." Extravagant birthday parties, expensive gifts, violent video games, mature movies, profane music and inappropriate clothing are just a few of the ways the world attempts to feed us a large helping of "compromise."

In the midst of this barrage, we can get distracted. When we look "to the right or to the left" at choices made by other parents or our children's friends, we open ourselves up to the pressures of conformity. We know where the truth lies, however. The trick is keeping our focus on Jesus.

Discipline yourself to focus on Jesus and His truth.

Weekend Reflection: Days 41 and 42

by Michelle Groff

> **How Original**
> A teacher in our Sunday School class for two-year-olds was looking through an animal picture book with a precocious little girl. The teacher would point to an animal and ask her what each animal says. When the teacher asked what a cow says, the child replied, "Eat more chicken."
> —Kim G.

The media has an incredible influence on our kids. Growing up, I was extremely jealous of a friend who was always on the cutting edge of "cool." She had the most fashionable clothes, the newest toys, and the trendiest makeup. From her Monkees spiral notebook to her Herbal Essence shampoo, if it was "in," she owned it. And I believed that if I owned the right stuff, I could be as popular as she was.

Unfortunately for me, my mother decided to try her hand at sewing when I was in the seventh grade. Let's just say her skills in this area were rudimentary at best. I didn't want to hurt her feelings, but I remember how mortified I was going to school day after day in versions of the same A-line dress that had one hole for my head, two holes for my arms, and one hole for my legs. Each dress was embellished with pockets, buttons or "rickrack," none of which were in style at the time.

When I had my two boys, I determined that they would not feel the embarrassment of such a fashion faux pas. But my efforts were not limited to their clothes. Whatever the marketing machines were selling for kids their age, I bought. Of course, I was acting out of my childhood insecurities. And,

Timeless Originals

sadly, some people judge us on how we look or what we wear. But instead of having conversations with my kids about having an identity that is secure in Christ, I was facilitating a store-bought identity that needed updating every few weeks.

There will always be people whose toys are cooler than ours. The best gift we can give our kids is to walk alongside them with empathy when they are tempted to accept cultural definitions of worth and remind them that as children of God, their value is never in question.

Even if they're wearing rickrack.

Notes

Week Seven

Day 43: Bible Study for Kids

But as for you, continue in what you have learned and have become convinced of, because you know those from whom you learned it, and how from infancy you have known the holy Scriptures, which are able to make you wise for salvation through faith in Christ Jesus (2 Tim. 3:14–15, NIV).

In this passage, we learn that Timothy had been raised in a godly home by a mother and grandmother who taught him the Scriptures. He had been surrounded by the Word "from infancy" in preparation for the time when Paul would lead him to salvation through Christ. This early immersion in the Word of God had prepared him for the message of Jesus.

It's never too early for your kids to start learning the Bible. In fact, the early years are some of the most productive, because your children will be excited to learn from you. There are excellent Bible storybooks with pictures for the very young and more sophisticated versions for older kids. Eventually, they can graduate to owning a Bible of their own.

So make an effort to lovingly introduce Scripture when your kids are young. This time doesn't last forever, and it will be a lot harder to do when they get into the teenage years. It is never too early to start a Bible study with your kids.

Timeless Originals

Day 44: Legacy

For I, the Lord your God, am a jealous God, punishing the children for the sin of the fathers to the third and fourth generation of those who hate me, but showing love to a thousand [generations] of those who love me and keep my commandments (Deut. 5:9–10, NIV).

God knows the consequences of sin, which is why He pleads for us to obey His commands. He lets us know in advance that our choices will have lasting consequences for us and for our children. Sinful choices can be the beginning of destructive family patterns that carry on generation after generation.

But God's mercy far outweighs His judgment. Many more generations will be blessed if we choose to love and obey Him. So, in the face of temptation, remember that the way we live our lives establishes a lasting legacy, either in the form of blessings or punishments. What will we choose to give our children and the generations that follow?

When faced with temptation, consider the legacy that sin passes on to your children.

Day 45: Answers to Prayer

This is the confidence we have in approaching God: that if we ask anything according to his will, he hears us. And if we know that he hears us—whatever we ask—we know that we have what we asked of him (1 John 5:14–15, NIV).

Parenting makes us doubt the truth of this passage like few other experiences. Because we love our children, we assume we know what is best for them. We pray for God to honor our plans and are shocked when He sometimes leads us down a more difficult path—one that includes testing and pain.

For me, the turning point came when I realized I was looking at God as a "cosmic vending machine." When I prayed, I somehow felt He was obligated to comply on my terms. Then a friend gave me a simple guide that changed my perspective on prayer. He said, "Prayer is asking God to align you with His will, rather than asking Him to be aligned with yours."

God knows what you and your children *really* need. When you pray, He is at work answering those prayers, but in a way that suits Him and His work. Faith trusts the wisdom of His answer, even when His answer is different from what you expect.

To truly pray for God's will to be done, you must trust that His will is what is best for your family.

Day 46: Humility

You may say to yourself, "My power and the strength of my hands have produced this wealth for me." But remember the Lord your God, for it is he who gives you the ability to produce wealth (Deut. 8:17–18, NIV).

Few things are more effective in undermining our walk with God than pride. Many of us claim to be dependent on Him, but live our lives depending on ourselves. The way we respond to both our achievements and our disappointments will be a powerful testimony to our children.

When our sense of worth soars with success, we are taking credit for positive results. However, such results ultimately depend on God, not on us. In His sovereign wisdom, He uses both good and bad experiences to bring about His plan. If we understand this, we will have a better perspective on success and failure.

Your talents are gifts from God, and while He calls you to use them for His glory, the outcome belongs to Him.

Model humility in your successes *and* your failures.

Day 47: Discipline with Empathy

Brothers, if someone is caught in a sin, you who are spiritual should restore him gently. But watch yourself, or you also may be tempted (Gal. 6:1–2, NIV).

Empathy is harder for some of us than it is for others. Learning to be more empathetic with our children may require us to take some time to remember what it was like when we were their age. Walking in their little shoes can help us understand why they do what they do. Sometimes we forget that we were children once, too.

Interestingly, we may find that the things we struggled with at their age cause us the most anxiety in parenting. We may be frustrated when the same issues reappear in our children. This remembrance can have two outcomes: (1) we might anxiously step in to fix the problem, which usually results in an overblown response and makes the situation worse; or (2) we might remember our experiences and use them to relate to our kids.

God may be using your child's struggles to sanctify both of you. So when your child's struggle causes you extraordinary anxiety, be alert—God may be teaching something to both of you.

Weekend Reflection: Days 48 and 49

by Michelle Groff

> **How Original**
> One evening, we had our extended family over for dinner, including great-grandparents, aunts and uncles. We asked our son to recite his full name for the family. He proudly said his first and last names. When I asked him to say his middle names as well, he quickly replied, "Oh, no. Those are my angry names."
> —Garnett K., age 3

I remember how excited I was when I found the inner strength to follow through in giving my boys consequences. Prior to that time, I had relied mostly on commands, threats, nagging, and reminding. But when it came time to deliver a consequence, I would wimp out. I don't know if I wanted to avoid their angry responses or if I just hated seeing them miss out on something they wanted to do. Either way, it didn't take much to change my mind. My boys will admit they had this down to an art form. Here's how it usually played out.

First, they would be extremely contrite, apologize, and promise never to do the offensive act again. If that didn't work, they would play the guilt card. They would say, "Everyone is going. We'll never have this chance again." Or they would whine, "We're going to be left behind," strongly hinting that being left behind would make them social outcasts and result in irreversible damage to their self-esteem.

I'm sad to report that these approaches were usually effective. However, if by some miracle neither one did the trick, they would move on to anger and the dreaded "silent treatment."

Timeless Originals

After a few hours, I was ready for them to be anywhere but in the house with me!

This pattern continued until our boys were in their late teens. At that point, Chris and I slowly began to stand our ground. It was a start, but the problem was the *way* we stood our ground. Now we were the angry ones. We resented having to follow through with a consequence because consequences were inconvenient! This resulted in "angry names" being tossed about like ping-pong balls in a bingo blower.

In addition, Chris and I were usually loud and defensive as we attempted to explain our reasons for giving them a consequence. We hoped our compelling lectures would lead them to renewed respect for our wisdom. Instead, we observed the molten lava of their emotions bubbling just beneath the surface. This made the atmosphere around our house very tense. There was an "us versus them" mentality that sapped the joy out of our time together.

Things finally started to change for the better when we realized we were leaving out the most important part of giving consequences: empathy. Simply put, empathy is a willingness to see a situation from the child's point of view and to acknowledge his or her thoughts and feelings. It doesn't require you to agree with the child's point of view, however. It sounds something like this: "I understand that you are really angry and disappointed about having to miss the party. I hope you make a better choice next time, because I know how much you enjoy being with your friends."

Empathy will require a unique kind of strength on your part. Not the overpowering, finger-pointing, steamrolling kind of strength, but the kind that will allow you to exercise your authority with calmness and consistency. This strength allows you to stay in control of yourself even when your kids are out of control. It will enable you to say, "I'm strong enough to hold you accountable for your poor choices without disconnecting from you. I might disagree with your actions, but your value isn't in question. And I'm interested in hearing your point of view."

Sounds a lot like our heavenly Father, doesn't it?

Notes

Week Eight

Day 50: Release Control

This day I call heaven and earth as witnesses against you that I have set before you life and death, blessings and curses. Now choose life, so that you and your children may live and that you may love the Lord your God, listen to his voice and hold fast to him (Deut. 30:19–20, NIV).

God does not force Himself on us. Even when the consequences are extremely severe, He gives us the choice to obey or disobey. How heartbreaking it must be when His children choose death over life.

Most of us can relate when we watch our kids make self-destructive choices for momentary pleasure. Every Christian parent yearns for his or her children to "choose life." Our example and the way we parent have an enormous influence on our kids, but neither will give us total control. Despite our best efforts, we must accept the fact that we cannot grant our kids an intimate relationship with the Lord. That is something they must choose for themselves.

Good parenting cannot guarantee a good result. For that, we must trust the Lord.

Day 51: Trust and Fear

Have I not commanded you? Be strong and courageous. Do not be terrified; do not be discouraged, for the Lord your God will be with you wherever you go (Josh. 1:9, NIV).

God spoke these words to Joshua as he was preparing for battle, but they are just as applicable to our lives today. The key to overcoming fear at work, in relationships, or in parenting is trust in God. Anyone who has raised a two-year-old or a teenager knows what it means to be terrified and discouraged! Yet God does not *ask* us to be courageous—He *commands* it.

How can we build the kind of faith that overcomes fear—fear that our kids will hurt or be hurt by others, fear that they will abuse alcohol or drugs, fear they will make sexual compromises, or fear that they will not come to know the Lord? The answer is to trust in God. This trust develops as we obey His Word and experience His love. We may not know God's purpose in many of our lives' events, but our peace comes from knowing Him.

Trust in God conquers fear in parenting.

Day 52: Stones of Remembrance

And Joshua set up at Gilgal the twelve stones they had taken out of the Jordan. He said to the Israelites, "In the future when your descendants ask their fathers, 'What do these stones mean?' Tell them, 'Israel crossed the Jordan on dry ground'" (Josh. 4:20–22, NIV).

This memorial of twelve stones was a great reminder to the Israelites of God's grace and power. When the Israelite children saw it, they would ask to hear the story and learn about

God. It kept God's faithfulness fresh in their parent's minds as well.

All of us have memories of answered prayers and of God's work in our lives. But how often do we share these stories with our children? When we are faced with trials, it can be easy to focus on our fear rather than on remembering how God has provided for us in the past.

Each time you experience God's grace, make a memorial of the occasion in your mind (you might even write it down). These are *your* stones of remembrance. Offer strength and encouragement by sharing your stories of God's faithfulness with your children.

Day 53: Confronting Rebellion

The Lord is slow to anger, abounding in love and forgiving sin and rebellion. Yet he does not leave the guilty unpunished (Num. 14:18, NIV).

What prevents you from calmly following through with consequences when your kids sin or rebel? I resisted giving consequences because I wanted to avoid angry responses such as, "Chill, mom!" or, "You're mean!" or, "I'll do it later." I tried reasoning with my kids, but this usually backfired. I tried arguing my point, but the more I talked, the angrier they seemed to become. I found I was hiding behind my words (nagging, reminding and arguing) to avoid giving consequences.

When you get an angry response for delivering consequences, don't escalate the situation by nagging or replying in anger. Words are easy. You may think that you are being "strong" when you argue your point forcefully or make dictatorial decrees, but the truth is that it takes more strength to hold your tongue and give consequences calmly and with empathy. That is a model of real strength.

Confront rebellion calmly and deliver consequences rather than words.

Day 54: Flexibility

And we urge you, brothers and sisters, admonish the undisciplined, comfort the discouraged, help the weak, be patient toward all (1 Thess. 5:14, NET).

Each of our children is unique. Some like lots of activities; others prefer time alone. Some are compliant; others constantly test the limits. Some have thick skins; others are easily offended. And each child will change over the years. As a result, our parenting approach depends on knowing our children and responding according to their unique personalities.

For the undisciplined or rebellious child, admonishment is needed. Parents of these children will be challenged to deliver consequences consistently and empathetically. For the discouraged child who is tempted to withdraw, comfort and encouragement are necessary. Parents of these children will need to learn to listen to their concerns and reflect their feelings back to them as they communicate confidence in their abilities. A weak child needs help. Maybe he or she tends toward adherence to "the rules" without understanding that there are principles *behind* the rules. Parents of these children can pass along spiritual wisdom by helping the child explore the reasons for his or her actions.

Regardless of your child's personality type, God asks you to be patient. God wants you to "know" each child and adapt your parenting style to each particular personality.

Week Eight

Weekend Reflection: Days 55 and 56

by Michelle Groff

> **How Original**
> Recently, my daughter came up to my pregnant belly, lifted up my shirt a bit, and asked, "Mom, can I talk to sister?"
> "Sure, sweetie," I said, touched by her tenderness in wanting to connect with her unborn sister.
> "Ha, ha, we just had cake and you didn't!"
> —S. H., age 3

A picture is worth a thousand words. As I leafed through a photo album, I came across an image of my sister Cynthia, my mom, and me in our Easter finery, complete with hats, gloves, and Dippity-Do hair. I was three years old and Cynthia was six. Despite the festive attire, the expression on my face indicated I was not a happy camper, and the picture reminded me why. If you looked carefully, you could see Cynthia's Easter basket was substantially larger than mine.

I'm sure my parents tried to explain why an older kid deserved a bigger basket, but, oh, the inhumanity! Forty-seven years later, I can still recall how jealous I was of my sister. But now, after having two boys, I empathize with my mother's predicament in having to deal with this kind of emotion before church on an Easter Sunday.

Few things are as exhausting to a parent as sibling rivalry. But if you think the situation at your home is unique, think again. The very first sibling relationship in history resulted in Cain killing Abel, and it didn't get much better from there. Jacob tricked Isaac into giving him Esau's blessing; Rachel and Leah competed for Jacob's love; Joseph's brothers sold him

Timeless Originals

into slavery; and when the prodigal son returned, his older brother was mad because his father threw a party.

Complicating the matter is the fact that one-size-fits-all parenting doesn't work well. God made each child unique. Children are born with different personalities, temperaments and abilities to handle responsibility. What is age-appropriate for one child may not be best for the other.

However, no matter how different our children are from one another, there is something they will need in equal measure: empathy. Empathy requires us to listen, to reflect their thoughts and feelings back to them, and to let them know we value their welfare over our convenience. Communicating with empathy fosters mutual understanding, teaches delayed gratification, and helps soften the blow when things can't be "fair."

But by all means, save yourself some unnecessary trouble. Get matching Easter baskets.

Notes

Week Nine

Day 57: Nagging

With such nagging she prodded him day after day until he was tired to death (Judg. 16:15–16, NIV).

Delilah nagged Samson until he finally revealed the secret of his strength. The phrase "tired to death" sums up the effects of nagging, doesn't it? Sometimes we give in to our kids' requests, even when we know it's not best for them, just to buy some momentary peace. It comes at a price, however, because when we do this, we've rewarded the very behavior we want to discourage.

Parents can be good at nagging, too. One reason we default to nagging is because it's easier than following through with consequences. But we have to ask ourselves whether relieving our anxiety for a moment is really producing the behavior we are seeking.

Our relationships with our children will suffer when we nag them. It's not a behavior that will earn their respect, and it can cause our kids to grow "tired to death" of us. Even though it's tough to give consequences with empathy, it's a much more considerate way to treat our children.

Giving consequences with empathy is far more effective than nagging.

Day 58: The Certainty of Our Hope

The Lord has taken away His judgments against you; He has cleared away your enemies. The King of Israel, the Lord, is in your midst; you will fear disaster no more (Zeph. 3:15).

We can live joyfully in the present when we know our future is secure. As Christian parents, we can approach the trials of life with calm assurance, because we know nothing on this earth can keep us from an eternity with God. As our kids experience disappointments—poor report cards, lost games, romantic breakups, fights with friends—we can pass along this message of hope.

Our faith is revealed in the way we respond to everyday events, yet sometimes we forget the end result that awaits those who trust in the Lord. We will live and reign with Christ. The future is assured.

In trials or in triumphs, rejoice in the hope of the coming age and pass that joy on to your children.

Day 59: The Power of Prayer

After this prayer, the meeting place shook, and they were all filled with the Holy Spirit. Then they preached the word of God with boldness (Acts 4:31, NLT).

In the early days of the Church, when the Christians faced problems, they turned to God in prayer and were rewarded with the power of the Holy Spirit. Imagine this scene. As the believers prayed, the room "shook" with the power of God!

Time after time, the Bible instructs us to pray and promises us that when we do, we will receive the power of the Spirit. Yet we often depend on our own strength to handle the problems of life, including parenting. How much easier it would be to surrender to God and rely on the Spirit to empower us to deal with our trials! It takes faith, however. A lack of faith causes us to rely on our own power rather than on the Holy Spirit.

Model a belief in the power of prayer and faith in God as you face parenting challenges.

Day 60: Maturing Spiritually

In fact, though by this time you ought to be teachers, you need someone to teach you the elementary truths of God's word all over again. You need milk, not solid food! Anyone who lives on milk, being still an infant, is not acquainted with the teaching about righteousness. But solid food is for the mature, who by constant use have trained themselves to distinguish good from evil (Heb. 5:12–14, NIV).

Carpools. Homework. Sports. Dance lessons. Our day is crammed with activities as we strive to meet the demands of parenting. But sometimes with all this activity we lose sight of the most important ingredient for godly parenting: nurturing our relationship with the living God.

Are you growing spiritually, or have you let everyday activities crowd out time for God? The greatest gift you can give your kids is the example of a deep relationship with God and a desire to know His truth. The "solid food" of spiritual maturity will overflow into your parenting as you tap into God's wisdom.

Grow in spiritual maturity by making it a priority to spend time with God.

Day 61: Quick to Listen, Slow to Speak

This you know, my beloved brethren. But everyone must be quick to hear, slow to speak and slow to anger; for the anger of man does not achieve the righteousness of God (James 1:19–20).

When we are faced with disrespectful, disobedient, or rebellious behavior from our children, it is natural for us to get angry. Unfortunately, this natural response is the least likely to uncover the heart issues that lie beneath that child's bad behavior. This is because the "anger of man" distracts us from a pursuit of righteousness. The anger of a parent confronted with a child's poor choice shifts the focus from the child's bad behavior to the parent's angry response.

These verses in James tell us to be quick to listen and slow to speak. Listening carefully, speaking little, and helping our children explore the motives behind their behavior can lead to the sort of insight that points them toward the righteousness of God.

Replace anger with empathy, and see what happens. Responding in this way is difficult, but the reward is great.

Week Nine

Weekend Reflection: Days 62 and 63

by Michelle Groff

> **How Original**
> When asking first-graders what they loved about our school, one child wrote, "I love school because it 'macs pepel smort!'"
> —Karen L., teacher

The road from childhood to maturity is paved with lots of mistakes. As parents who see the world from an adult perspective, we can forget what it's like to be a kid. This is especially true during the teen years. When my boys started to *look* like adults, I assumed they could *think* like adults. But then they would ...

- Wear potholders instead of shoes on their feet

- Make a hammock out of sheets and suspend a friend over the staircase

- Dare a friend to eat a roach

- Build a campfire inside a wooden fort

In response, I pointed out the immaturity of their thinking (usually through sarcasm). Although my goal was to teach them a lesson and help them avoid future suffering, they felt as if I were trying to expose them as idiots or prove my superior intelligence.

Nobody likes to feel that someone is trying to expose his or her flaws. Being under our authority puts children in a vulnerable position because we can use that authority in ways

Timeless Originals

that belittle and shame them. But notice how God responded to Adam and Eve when they ate the forbidden fruit in the Garden of Eden. He didn't yell "gotcha!" or say sarcastically, "Hey, Adam! How do you like the taste of that special fruit?" Instead, He asked questions that encouraged self-exploration: "Adam, where are you? Who told you that you were naked?" He stayed connected, and even as He gave them the consequences they earned, He covered their shame with animal skins.

The way we respond to our kids' mistakes will stay with them for years to come. So the next time you are tempted to be condescending or sarcastic, try to remember what it was like to be a kid. Stay calm. Ask questions, and listen before talking. Be empathetic, even as you're giving consequences.

When you focus on being respectful in exercising your authority, you will find it is a much more effective way to "mac pepel smort."

Notes

Week Ten

Day 64: Stewardship

Now Joseph had been taken down to Egypt; and Potiphar, an Egyptian officer of Pharaoh, the captain of the bodyguard, bought him from the Ishmaelites ... So Joseph found favor in his sight and he made him overseer over his house, and ... he left everything he owned in Joseph's charge; and with him there he did not concern himself with anything except the food which he ate (Gen. 39:1–6).

Joseph was a good steward. Although he didn't own anything in Potiphar's house, his master entrusted him to manage everything in it. Joseph never laid claim to Potiphar's possessions, but he managed Potiphar's affairs well, knowing that one day he would be accountable for the results.

Don't forget that you have been given *stewardship* over your children, rather than *ownership*. They belong to God, but He has entrusted you with their care and growth while they are under your care. How might this perspective affect the way you parent?

Children belong to God, and you are God's steward over them.

Timeless Originals

Day 65: To Know and Be Known

I am ready to come to you, and I will not be a burden to you; for I do not seek what is yours, but you; for children are not responsible to save up for their parents, but parents for their children (2 Cor. 12:14).

What do we seek from our children? Sometimes we seek validation from their achievements. It feels good to be the parent of an overachieving child. In the end, however, if we seek to be validated by their acts, we are seeking what is *theirs*. Instead, we should be seeking *them*. Our kids are not responsible for our well being; we are responsible for theirs.

Think of your relationship to your heavenly Father. God does not need your performance; He wants only you. To be known by God despite your faults and failings is your highest reward (see Matt. 7:23), and it is no different for your children. They long to be known by you for their own merit, not for their ability to perform. To model that kind of love for your children is to model the love that God has for us.

Seek to "know" your children for who God made them to be.

Day 66: Talking About God

Fix these words of mine in your hearts and minds. … Teach them to your children, talking about them when you sit at home and when you walk along the road, when you lie down and when you get up (Deut. 11:18–19, NIV).

Is God a part of your everyday conversation with your kids, or do spiritual topics feel forced and awkward? What you truly value will be revealed in how you spend your time and money and in your words. Is your passion for God as obvious as your passion for sports, good grades, or vacations?

When we share God's wisdom moment-by-moment, carpool-by-carpool, or breakfast-by-breakfast, the lessons of the Bible come alive. Life provides countless opportunities for us to illustrate the truth of God's Word to our children. When we demonstrate that He is relevant and vital to our everyday lives, we encourage our children to write this truth on their hearts as well.

Demonstrate your love for God by talking with your kids about His influence in your everyday life.

Day 67: Looking Heavenward

Therefore if you have been raised up with Christ, keep seeking the things above, where Christ is, seated at the right hand of God. Set your mind on the things above, not on the things that are on earth (Col. 3:1–2).

In parenting, our discontent and pride can reveal areas where we get caught up in the "things that are on earth." We can be competitive when we compare our children to other kids. We feel validated when they are the star athlete or an academic whiz, and we get upset when they are overlooked or are unmotivated. We find ourselves buying into the value system of other parents.

How can you set your mind on things above? Start the day by praising God. Ask Him to reveal your motivations. Recognize where you are seeking the approval of others over the approval of God. Seek His wisdom through Bible study and prayer. God provides the resources, but you "set your

Timeless Originals

mind on things above" when you incorporate those resources into your parenting.

Make a conscious effort each day to focus on what is eternally important.

Day 68: Delivering Consequences

But the Lord said to Moses and Aaron, "Because you did not trust in me enough to honor me as holy in the sight of the Israelites, you will not bring this community into the land I give them" (Num. 20:12, NIV).

Talk about a tough consequence! Moses, the great leader of the Exodus and giver of God's laws, was not allowed to enter the Promised Land because he disobeyed God. Moses pleaded with the Lord to change His mind, but God followed through with the consequence.

Even great leaders and great kids can make serious errors. In a culture of declining moral standards, following through with the right consequences can feel unloving and harsh. But helping our children develop habits of obedience requires us to establish clear boundaries and consistently enforce the consequences when they disobey.

Though it may seem harsh, delivering consequences consistently is an act of love.

Week Ten

Weekend Reflection: Days 69 and 70

by Michelle Groff

> **How Original**
> Our five-year-old daughter knocked on our bedroom door at 5 a.m., complaining that her foot itched. Her dad said, "Scratch it and go to bed." She replied, "When momma comes, she scratches it and kisses me." Her dad responded, "I'm not momma." She then said, "Close the door and I'll knock again, but this time let momma get up."
> —Macy B, age 5

One time before we became parents, Chris and I were eating lunch with another couple and their five-year-old daughter, April. As we were waiting to be seated at the restaurant, April asked if she could have some of the chocolate mints that were in a bowl for people to take on their way out. Her mom said, "No, honey, we're about to eat lunch, and I don't want you to ruin your appetite." April, however, wasn't interested in "no" for an answer. Like Chinese water torture, she kept asking and asking. Finally, our friends relented and let her have the mints. I remember thinking to myself, *I would never let my child act like that!*

Famous last words.

My boys were quick learners. They became experts at detecting the chinks in Chris's and my defenses. Like Las Vegas gamblers, they played the odds. I pictured them sitting around with their friends as they determined the over/under on parental responses: "Okay, what are the odds our moms will cave in and give us what we want to avoid an embarrassing scene in a public place? I'm gonna go with 3 to 1. Except for your mom, Alex. She's been tough to beat recently.

Timeless Originals

Now, we don't need to worry about being able to postpone bedtime by making random requests. That's a no-brainer. But getting junk food for a late afternoon snack is tricky, because of that nutrition thing."

I totally underestimated how much energy it would require to be consistent in my discipline. With schedules jam-packed with activities, it was much easier to accommodate my boys' demands than it was to muster the physical and emotional reserve needed to provide a firm boundary. Not to mention the inconvenience—leaving a party early, requiring kids to do their chores instead of doing them myself, taking time to listen to their point of view even when I disagreed, or adopting a schedule that didn't push me to my absolute limit.

But when I look at the life of Jesus, I see a model of calm consistency. He had a way of listening that made people feel deeply known, yet He didn't compromise truth for the sake of convenience. Even as the crowds clamored for His attention, He made it a priority to refresh His spirit by spending time with the Father.

Sometimes we forget that we have the same resource from which we can draw. God calls us to depend on Him as we acknowledge the limits of our wisdom and resources. And we will always find limits there for our protection.

Sounds like a model worth imitating.

Notes

Week Eleven

Day 71: Eternal Perspective

For our light and momentary troubles are achieving for us an eternal glory that far outweighs them all. So we fix our eyes not on what is seen, but on what is unseen. For what is seen is temporary, but what is unseen is eternal (2 Cor. 4:17–18, NIV).

God never wastes suffering. Our trials work for us, not against us (see James 1:2–5). If we trust God and surrender to Him, the trials we endure will produce patience, perseverance, and maturity in the lives of our family. However, if we rebel and fight against our circumstances, we will remain impatient, impulsive and immature. God allows trials so He can build character into our lives. Warren Wiersbe gives a great analogy: "God can grow a mushroom overnight, but it takes many years—and many storms—to build a mighty oak."

It takes an eternal perspective to see beyond today to eternity, and your kids are not likely to be able to do it without your gentle, guiding hand. As you empathetically walk through trials with them, you can model the faith, hope and love that will allow them to look at tough situations as opportunities to grow, develop and become more like Christ.

An eternal perspective will give you the ability to see beyond temporary trials.

Day 72: Being the Ultimate Example

But God had mercy on me so that Christ Jesus could use me as a prime example of his great patience with even the worst sinners. Then others will realize that they, too, can believe in him and receive eternal life (1 Tim. 1:16, NLT).

Kids learn some of the most important lessons by watching the most influential people in their lives: their parents. They learn by watching our example in good times and bad. In the bad times, when we act with anger, ridicule, condescension or selfishness, we will have an extra opportunity to model the humility that results from confession and repentance and the mercy and grace that comes from being a child of God.

As your children grow, they will see that you are not perfect. Hopefully, they will seek the source of perfection in the only place it can be found: God. You can show them the way by demonstrating that the best response to imperfections is to present them to God with a grateful heart, knowing that His mercy and grace will wipe the slate clean. What an opportunity to communicate the gospel message to your kids in a practical, real-life manner.

Be an example of God's patience, mercy and grace. Your kids are watching.

Day 73: Anger

Be angry, and yet do not sin; do not let the sun go down on your anger, and do not give the devil an opportunity (Eph. 4:26–27).

Anger is not always wrong; it's what we do with our anger that will determine whether we are acting righteously or sinfully. We *should* be angered by acts of ungodliness, unrighteousness, injustice, and inequity. These things anger God as well. But if we are angry because someone has disturbed our pride, self-sufficiency, status, prestige or power, then our reaction will likely be sinful. Sinful anger is often expressed in harshness, cruelty, bitterness and a lack of self-control.

You must always examine your heart when your kids make you angry. If it is righteous anger, then let it motivate you to take action and deliver consequences. Sin needs to be addressed, and you will honor God by delivering those consequences with empathy and love. However, if it is sinful anger, then pray for the courage to confess it, repent and resolve it.

Examine your anger to determine the motives behind it.

Day 74: Sacrifice

Then he reached out his hand and took the knife to slay his son. But the angel of the Lord called out to him from heaven, "Abraham! Abraham!" (Gen. 22:10–11, NIV).

When we read this story, we marvel at Abraham's willingness to sacrifice his only son. Yet many of us are willing to sacrifice our children as well—not out of obedience to the Lord, but to the expectations of this world. This sacrifice requires no knife but is executed in subtle day-to-day compromises. Overcrowded schedules that squeeze out time for relationships. Messages that communicate to our children that their significance is determined by success. Pressuring our kids to perform because we see them as a reflection of ourselves. Investing our time and money chasing after power, beauty, and fame.

We are bombarded with false messages that define the worth of our children by worldly standards. Like Abraham, God is calling us to bring this sacrifice to a halt. But we must look past the temporal and see with eternal eyes. We must choose to worship the Creator instead of the creation.

Surrender your kids to God and spend the time necessary to uncover His plan for their lives.

Day 75: Good Boundaries

You must obey my laws and be careful to follow my decrees. I am the Lord your God. Keep my decrees and laws for the man who obeys them will live by them (Lev. 18:4–5, NIV).

The laws given to the Israelites may seem overwhelming and tedious to us. God's requirements covered everything from priestly duties to skin care! But this was not an exercise in excessive control. The Israelite community was beginning a journey into the wilderness, and God knew the pitfalls and temptations that lay ahead. These regulations were a gesture of His love and grace to help them succeed as a nation.

Similarly, we know the pitfalls that await our children on their journey to adulthood, so we establish reasonable boundaries out of our love for them and our desire to protect them. We know that they do not have the maturity and wisdom to set limits for themselves.

When you find it difficult to hold fast to your boundaries, remember God's example with the Israelites. Firm boundaries communicate love and promote security. Good boundaries let your children know you love them.

Weekend Reflection: Days 76 and 77

by Michelle Groff

> **How Original**
> I had set a consequence for my daughter: no TV for two days. That evening, we were at her brother's middle school band concert and she was keeping herself busy by writing. Here's what she wrote: "Mom, I love you. You are sweet to me even when you said I couldn't watch TV. Daddy married the right woman, and that would be you, my mom."
> —M.H., age 7

Our therapist partner, Lee Long, is constantly amazed when kids come into his counseling office and tell him that they wish their parents would set boundaries for them. Teenagers admitting they need limits? Isn't that against their job description? Absolutely! That's why they ask Lee not to tell their parents that the idea came from them.

As a parent, this may perplex you. After all, most teenagers spend the better part of their day arguing against boundaries. But deep inside, they crave them. Limits demonstrate to them that their parents love them enough to set guidelines for how they should behave. In fact, studies consistently confirm that kids who are raised by permissive or neglectful parents develop many more psychological issues than those who are not.

Sometimes our kids' emotional turmoil can be tough on us. I had a tendency to take it personally when my boys got angry at the boundaries I set. I expected them to understand, and when they didn't, my feelings were hurt. Sometimes I would be lenient in order to avoid conflict, while other times I would overcompensate by blasting them with commands and lectures.

Timeless Originals

It takes wisdom and patience to learn to control our emotions when our kids can't control theirs. A friend of Lee's who was adopted shared that when she was in her teens, her mother set a boundary that made her furious. She yelled, "I hate you!" With tears in her eyes, her mother responded, "I love you so much that I'm willing to do what's best for you even if it means you hate me."

Lee's friend says that was the moment she no longer felt adopted.

Notes

Week Twelve

Day 78: Need for Rest

The apostles gathered together with Jesus; and they reported to Him all that they had done and taught. And He said to them, "Come away by yourselves to a secluded place and rest a while" (Mark 6:30–31).

Christ sent the disciples out in twos on their first mission trip to preach the kingdom of God and cast out demons and heal the sick. Their trips were enormously successful, and they returned to Christ to report what had happened. The people around them were also apparently aware of the disciples' success, because they were so besieged by requests for their time that they had no time even to eat.

Imagine the feeling of being flushed with success and having people clamoring for your attention and begging for a little of your time. It had to feel pretty good to be needed like that. Yet Jesus recognized that boundaries were necessary to prevent the disciples from getting depleted. They needed time to rest.

You are no different. Your kids may demand every minute of your time, and it may feel pretty good to be needed that much. But you must be aware that you are limited in energy; you will be no good to anyone if you don't get some rest now and then.

Taking time to rest and revitalize is as important to your kids as it is to you.

Day 79: Hypocrisy

But there is nothing covered up that will not be revealed, and hidden that will not be known (Luke 12:2).

Fear of man will prove to be a snare, but whoever trusts in the Lord is kept safe (Prov. 29:25, NIV).

How often does fear drive you to do something you shouldn't? Fear can be driven by a need for approval from others, a need for control, envy of another person's lifestyle, or concern about being left behind by your peer group's march to "success." These fears are summed up in the concept of "fear of man."

The Bible tells us that fear of man will prove to be a snare because it is a substitute for fear of God. When we are overly concerned about our standing before others, we will strive for worldly things rather than godly ones. This striving is not hidden from God. He sees our hearts and knows the fear that motivates us. We may try to justify our efforts to gain approval, control or a better lifestyle as advancements to be used for God's work, but He knows the real fear that motivates us.

The remedy for hypocrisy is to fear God alone.

Week Twelve

Day 80: Worry

And which of you by worrying can add a single hour to his life's span? If then you cannot do even a very little thing, why do you worry about other matters? (Luke 12:25–26).

Do you worry? Most of us do, and yet Jesus tells us clearly we have nothing to worry about. In fact, He tells us it is counterproductive. We don't need to worry, because we know how our story will end. If our hope is assured (see Heb. 11:1), we shouldn't be concerned about the sorrows of today or tomorrow. "Worry does not empty tomorrow of its sorrow," said Corrie ten Boom, "it empties today of its strength."

How do we inoculate ourselves against worry? The answer is faith. When our hearts are fixed on God, we see life from an eternal viewpoint. We are able to put God's goals first. The question we must keep asking is, "Where is my heart?" If our hearts are fixed on worldly things, we will always worry, because the world's treasures are uncertain. However, if our hearts are fixed on God, we will rest in His power and strength.

Great faith can cancel out worry.

Day 81: Anticipating Christ's Return

Be like men who are waiting for their master when he returns from the wedding feast, so that they may immediately open the door to him when he comes and knocks. Blessed are those slaves whom the master will find on the alert when he comes; truly I say to you, that he will gird himself to serve, and have them recline at the table, and will come up and wait on them (Luke 12:36–37).

In Jesus' time, Jewish weddings were held at night. Because of this, a bridegroom's servants would anxiously wait for their

Timeless Originals

master to come home. They wanted to be ready so they didn't keep the new husband and his bride waiting at the door. Jesus used this illustration to show how believers should likewise enthusiastically anticipate and prepare for His return.

As we raise our kids, it is easy to focus on the here and now rather than the things of heaven. The issues of the moment—potty training, homework, being in the starting lineup, choosing a college—can cause us to lose sight of our real purpose on earth. Instead of preparing for our Master's return, we often choose to serve ourselves instead. However, when we live with our eyes on the eternal, it is more difficult for the things of the world to ensnare us.

Show your kids an example of the freedom that comes when you filter your experiences through an eternal perspective. Be an example of someone serving the Lord and waiting anxiously for His return.

Day 82: True Value

The king of Egypt said to the Hebrew midwives, whose names were Shiprah and Puah, "When you help the Hebrew women in childbirth and observe them on the delivery stool, if it is a boy, kill him; but if it is a girl, let her live" (Exod. 1:15, NIV).

The Hebrew midwives in this story feared God and did not obey the king's request. Interestingly, the Bible records the names of the midwives, but not the name of the Egyptian king. By worldly standards, this doesn't make sense. Egyptian kings were far more "important" than Hebrew midwives. But people who are revered on earth don't necessarily possess the qualities that are celebrated by God.

Week Twelve

It is so easy to crave validation, status, and notoriety for our kids. We are tempted to buy into our culture's definition of "success." God's plan for our kids, however, may not bring worldly fame. Even so, we should rejoice because there is no greater blessing than raising kids who are faithful to their calling.

Are you encouraging your kids to be significant to the world or to God?

Timeless Originals

Weekend Reflection: Days 83 and 84

by Michelle Groff

> **How Original**
> Because our daughter adored her older brother, she preferred to be associated with boys rather than girls. When ordering at restaurants, she would not let us order a "girl cheese" (grilled cheese). Instead, she wanted a "boy cheese."
>
> —A.S., age 3

Early on, kids learn the world's view that image is everything. But, of course, they're not the only ones.

When my youngest son entered kindergarten, I took up tennis and promptly bought all the appropriate gear: tennis dresses, racquets, racquet bag, shoes, and socks. After eight years of raising two preschool boys, putting on tennis clothes instantly made me feel younger, healthier, and more athletic, even before I set foot on the court. I liked the idea of being identified as a "tennis player" and longed for my skills to match the new image I had embraced.

That, however, would require a lot of practice, so I took lessons, attended drills, and entered a league where I played against other players of my skill level. Pretty soon a disturbing trend emerged: If I won a match, I felt validated; but if I lost, I couldn't wait for the next chance to redeem myself. Bit by bit, my sense of worth became increasingly tied to winning. And, judging by the questionable line calls made by some of my opponents, I wasn't alone.

Week Twelve

As I started hearing God's call for my life, I began to reevaluate my priorities. Then I was diagnosed with multiple sclerosis and had to give up tennis altogether. This led to an identity crisis and lots of self-reflection as I realized how much I depended on tennis to define me.

It's easy to fall into this trap. Our society idolizes success, and people cling to a myriad of identities to validate themselves: the "good cook," the "responsible mother," the "successful businessman" and the "Bible study leader" are just a few. If we're not careful, we can saddle our kids with performance-based identities as well: the "good student," the "great athlete," the "cheerleader" and the "talented musician." When we become too focused on achievements, our kids may find it hard to accept the simplicity of God's unconditional love.

We have value because we are made in the image of God. Our sins are forgiven through faith in Jesus Christ. It's that simple. No top ten percent and no impressive résumé required. Just grace.

> But we all, with unveiled face, beholding as in a mirror the glory of the Lord, are being transformed into the same image from glory to glory, just as from the Lord, the Spirit.
> —2 Corinthians 3:18

Come to think of it, I guess image really is everything after all.

Notes

Week Thirteen

Day 85: Wait

I would have lost heart, unless I had believed that I would see the goodness of the Lord in the land of the living. Wait on the Lord; be of good courage, and He shall strengthen your heart; wait, I say, on the Lord! (Ps. 27:13–14, NKJV).

Twenty-four hours a day. Seven days a week. We are constantly called to make parenting decisions on the fly. The pressure can be overwhelming. In the process, our nerves and faith are tested.

Perhaps this passage is most applicable when the demands are the greatest. It takes courage to wait on the Lord when our mind is screaming to *"do something!"* But until God has strengthened our heart, our actions will be impulsive and ineffective.

Instead of relying on your own snap judgments, trust in the goodness of God and wait for His guidance. He will supply you with the strength and wisdom you need (Heb. 13:20–21). When you are under pressure, be patient and wait for the Lord to strengthen your heart and guide your actions.

Day 86: The Example of Spending

We want to avoid any criticism of the way we administer this liberal gift. For we are taking pains to do what is right, not only in the eyes of the Lord but also in the eyes of men (2 Cor. 8:20–21, NIV).

The Macedonians had given money to Paul to give to the believers in Jerusalem. In this passage, Paul acknowledges the importance of spending that money responsibly. He knew that people were watching, and he wanted to be sure his actions were above reproach.

Think about how this applies to parenting. Your kids witness practical demonstrations of faith when they see you studying the Bible or praying. But they are also watching and learning from the way you spend your money. You may not realize what a powerful testimony your spending can be and how much it reveals about the things you treasure.

Jesus said, "Where your treasure is, there your heart will be also" (Matt. 6:21). So take some time to pray and consider what your lifestyle and spending communicates to your kids. Your faith will be prominently displayed by the way you spend the wealth God has given you.

Day 87: Knowledge versus Wisdom

Where is the wise man? Where is the scribe? Where is the debater of this age? Has not God made foolish the wisdom of the world? For since in the wisdom of God the world through its wisdom did not come to know God, God was well-pleased through the foolishness of the message preached to save those who believe (1 Cor. 1:20–21).

The education of our children can be an all-consuming passion. We struggle to get them into the right schools, starting with preschool, and continuing through graduate school. But we must keep in mind that a great education does not guarantee success in God's eyes. Many of today's schools, particularly colleges, consider the message of the cross "foolish." To them it is a sign of weakness, disgrace and low standing. As parents, we must counter that message with the truth that the world's wisdom will not save them. The greatest secular education misses the point: only the cross can save.

Wisdom is available when you seek God. When you concentrate your efforts on teaching your children the value of an eternal perspective, you can worry a little less about the world's view of where wisdom can be found.

Day 88: Love of the World

Do not love the world or the things in the world. If anyone loves the world, the love of the Father is not in him. For all that is in the world, the lust of the flesh and the lust of the eyes and the boastful pride of life, is not from the Father, but is from the world (1 John 2:15–16).

Is there a more important lesson we can teach our children? Pursuit of material things never satisfies, and it never ends. God has much more for us than the things we desire here on earth.

Unfortunately, we often live in such a way that our kids cannot see this truth. They see us striving and stressing because we have one thing but want something more. They see us comparing ourselves to others. Sadly, they may even see us comparing *them* to other kids and pushing them to be "successful" in school, athletics and relationships.

Is love of the "things in the world" your example to your kids? How can you better demonstrate a love of spiritual things?

Day 89: Childlike, but Not Childish

I tell you the truth, anyone who will not receive the kingdom of God like a little child will never enter it (Luke 18:17, NIV).

Perhaps part of the reason God gives us children is so we can see Him more clearly. The way our children relate to us gives us unique insights into the way we relate to our Father. When our children give us a drawing, inexpert as it may be, we hang it on our refrigerator or office wall. It's the motivation we treasure, not the execution. If our kids' gifts give us that much joy, imagine how God must feel when we offer gifts to Him with hearts motivated by love.

Likewise, when our children act selfishly, rebelliously, or disobediently, we get a glimpse of the other side of our relationship with our Father. The pain we feel when our children rebel cannot compare with the pain of our Father, for whom the stakes are much higher.

We can learn a lot about God from our relationship with our kids, and we should emulate their best characteristics when we relate to our heavenly Father. A loving child exhibits humility, faith, dependence, and a sense of wonder that makes life exciting. A rebellious child is selfish, petty, and disobedient.

Jesus instructs us to be *childlike*, but not *childish*. The loving child is a model for our relationship with God.

Week Thirteen

Weekend Reflection: Day 90

by Michelle Groff

> **How Original**
> "Give a man a fish; you have fed him for today. Teach a man to fish; and you have fed him for a lifetime."
> —Author unknown

One summer, Chris and I took a trip to Colorado to try our hands at fly-fishing for the first time. We had taken a beginner's course in Fort Worth, and I was confident that I would be able to execute my new skills with at least a modest measure of success. Chris had arranged for a fishing guide, James, to help us out.

When the big day came, we eagerly jumped into our guide's truck. I had all the gear in tow, including my polarized sunglasses that were supposed to help me see the fish under the water. When we reached the river, I waded in and attempted to wow James with my dexterity and skill at casting. This was virtually impossible, because I possessed neither. I quickly became frustrated.

James had been guiding this river for many years. It was "catch and release" fishing, and he was so familiar with the territory that he actually had names for the fish. I felt sorry for him that he had to endure my rudimentary efforts. Besides a lack of skill, my biggest problem was that I just plain couldn't see the fish. Here was James, excitedly greeting his fish friends: "Hey, look, there's Sam!" "Hello there, Julie." "What's up, Norton?" It started to grate on my nerves. Where were these stinking fish? I squinted and strained with all my might, but all I could see was murky, greenish water. One thing I knew for sure: I wanted a refund on my polarized glasses.

Timeless Originals

James watched me with amusement. As he saw my frustration escalate, he realized he needed to intervene before I went "postal" on him. He came alongside me, took my arm, and proceeded to do an amazing job of casting toward the various fish *he* could see just below the surface. One trout (I think it was Norton) took the fly. As James set the hook, he exclaimed with great excitement, "You caught a fish!"

I hated to burst James's bubble, but *I* had caught nothing. *James* had caught the fish, and he had managed to do it with the pole attached to the arm of a middle-aged housewife. Did he actually think I was duped into believing that I had made any contribution toward getting that fish on the line?

James wanted me to be happy in my accomplishment, but actually I was irritated with him. What I really wanted James to do was to spend some time teaching me how to *see* the fish. What exactly should I be looking for? Where do they like to hang out? What subtleties differentiate fish from rocks?

It dawned on me that this story is an analogy for our role in parenting. How often do we feel compelled to intervene and "do the fishing" for our kids? We see their struggles. We have the answers. We've fished these waters before. We know the fish by name, and we know exactly how to navigate the murky water that seems so foreign to our children. We hate to see their frustration and failure. And, after all, we know how to catch the fish.

The problem is, as frustrated as our children may be, they don't really want us to catch the fish for them. What they really want (and need) is for us to help them see the fish for themselves so they can catch them on their own.

So often, we misinterpret frustration as a plea to intervene on behalf of our kids. Our efforts to help them see the fish

Week Thirteen

become distorted, and we end up addressing our needs more than theirs. We might rescue them by taking their arm and doing the casting for them. We might criticize their lack of discipline and tell them, at length, how we learned to be so adept in our fishing skills. We might get exasperated and choose to sit in the truck, secretly hoping they'll recognize their need for us (and our great wisdom), and beg us to come back into the river. Or we might resent the fact that we're not going to be able to tell our friends back at the lodge just how successful we were in teaching our children how to fish, and what talented fishermen they turned out to be.

What can we do to avoid these pitfalls and help our children see the fish? We can sit patiently in the river with them as they flail and grumble and learn. We can restrain the urge to do the fishing for them. We can wait for them to ask for our guidance instead of suffocating them with our "knowledge." We can choose well-timed words of encouragement over lectures. We can avoid the trap of seeing their success or failures as reflections on us. And we can value the process of learning over the final result. If we can quell the storm within us as parents, the payoff will be precious indeed. Lo and behold, our child might start to catch a glimpse of those fish.

What are the various "fish" that we are trying to help them see? Perhaps it is setting an alarm to get up on time. Maybe it's realizing that studying cannot be left until the night before a major exam. It could be that failing a class means repeating a grade. Perhaps it is earning money to buy a car.

Of course, those are the easy fish. What about lessons on how to deal with a so-called friend who offers drugs? That drinking and driving endangers innocent lives? That lying undermines trust in any relationship? That hard work and delayed gratification are tough on the front end, but pay big dividends later on? How about the fact that respect is

Timeless Originals

earned, and true friends are treasured gifts? That choices in life demand personal responsibility, and those choices can greatly affect the quality of life?

A funny thing happens when we teach our kids to see their own fish: we start to see fish in our own lives that have been camouflaged in the murky waters! Some of us have spent a lifetime avoiding those fish. We don't want to see them, because doing so requires painful self-examination and introspection. Seeing those fish demands an honest assessment on our part of what we say we value in life versus what is really consuming our time, energy, and thoughts. These fish may take the form of pride or a desire for control, comfort or security. They may be a need to be right or validated by others. Or they may be a willingness to worship the creation over the Creator.

The beautiful thing is that just as we are trying to help our kids see their fish, we have a heavenly Parent who is working to help us see our own fish as well. He is dutifully with us in the river of life as we grumble and flail. He gives us freedom to make our own choices—even poor ones—and learn from the consequences. He whispers words of encouragement and love in our ears, but He doesn't force us to do things His way. He promises never to go sit in the truck, or, worse, drive away. He gives us room to learn tough lessons about our misplaced affections and ourselves. And He rejoices with us each time we catch a flicker of that elusive fish and welcomes us into His celebratory embrace.

Notes

About the Authors

Chris Groff is the executive director of Parenting by Design and is a regular Parenting by Design seminar speaker. He is the co-author of four parenting books and the workbook that accompanies the Parenting by Design Principles & Practice small-group study. Chris and his wife, Michelle, felt called to establish Parenting by Design with therapist Lee Long after finding God's provision in the midst of difficult challenges involving their children. Chris has a Master's Degree in Christian Education from Dallas Theological Seminary. He and Michelle have been married since 1981 and have two sons, Ben and Bob.

Michelle Groff, MA, LPC Intern, is co-founder of Parenting by Design and leads Parenting by Design seminars with her husband, Chris. She is a contributor to the Parenting by Design curriculum and is a frequent speaker on parenting issues in churches and schools. Michelle has a Master's Degree in Biblical Counseling from Dallas Theological Seminary, and is a Licensed Professional Counselor Intern in the state of Texas.

Charlotte Long is married to Lee Long. She is a contributor to *Timeless Originals* and has a Bachelor's Degree in Communications from the University of Texas. Charlotte spent most of her career teaching, and currently works full-time raising their three kids, Ella, Molly, and Rhodes. Charlotte's role as "Mom" has been honored in numerous prominent art pieces, including finger paint, glued macaroni, and play dough.

Parenting Resources from Parentingbydesign.com

Principles & Practice 8-Disk DVD Kit for individuals or small groups

Discover real, practical parenting help through this informative DVD seminar series. The special 8-DVD set includes the entire *Principles & Practice* seminar and two workbooks. The small-group set also includes a leader's guide and 10 participant workbooks.

$99.00
individual set

$199.00
small group set
plus shipping and handling

Principles & Practice online course

Containing the same information given at our live seminars, the *Principles & Practice* online course will give you a biblical guide to raising spiritually and emotionally healthy children. The best part is that you can enjoy the course on your schedule and for a fraction of the cost at www.parentingbydesign.com.

$59.00

Principles & Practice CD Kit

Discover real, practical parenting help through this informative CD seminar series. The special 8-CD set includes the entire *Principles & Practice* seminar.

$59.00 + shipping and handling

Six Parenting Essentials for the Busy Dad booklet & CD set

In this CD and booklet combo set, Parenting by Design founders, Chris Groff and Lee Long, give busy dads the basic principles they need to improve their parenting skills. Set includes an 80-page booklet and 80-minute CD.

$15.00 + shipping and handling

10 Keys to Successful Parenting CD

In this informational CD, Chris Groff shares 10 practical things you can do to focus on God's definition of successful parenting in a world that has the "success" thing all wrong.

$10.00 + shipping and handling

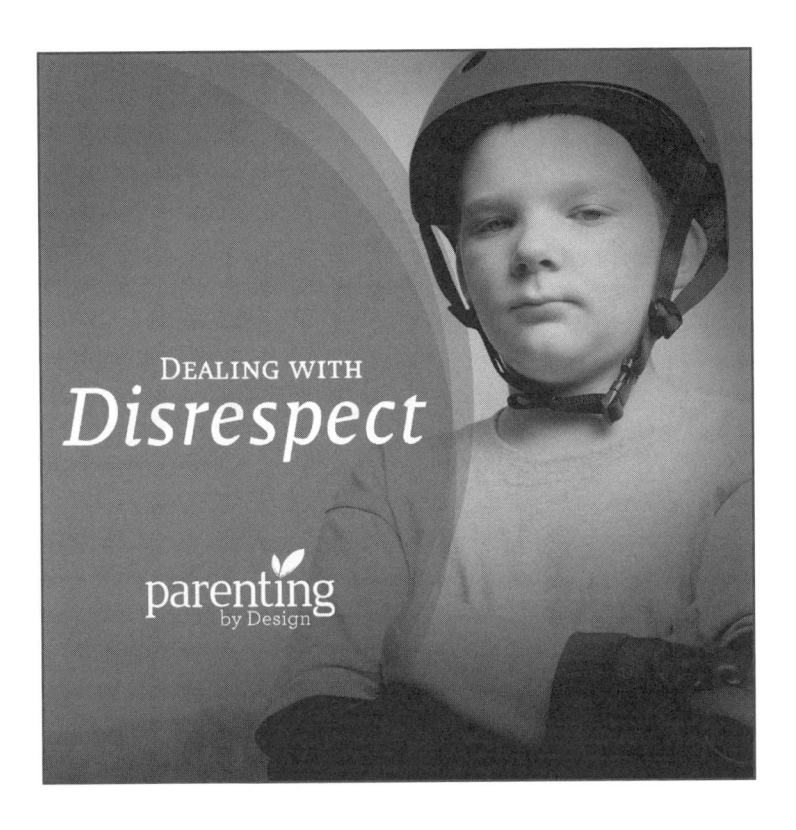

Dealing with Disrespect CD

If you have trouble keeping your cool when your children are disrespectful, you're not alone! This teaching CD will help you determine the difference between normal objections and disrespect and will help you effectively deal with both.

$10.00 + shipping and handling

Understanding Conflict with Your Children CD

This special teaching CD will help you understand the dynamics behind child-parent struggles and give you some important tips in resolving major and minor conflicts in your home.

$10.00 + shipping and handling

To order these and other helpful parenting resources, visit us at www.parentingbydesign.com/store *or call toll-free (877) 357-2112.*

If you are interested in having Chris and Michelle Groff come speak at your church or school, please e-mail info@parentingbydesign.com.

WinePressPublishing
Great Books, Defined.

To order additional copies of this book call:
1-877-421-READ (7323)
or please visit our website at
www.WinePressbooks.com

If you enjoyed this quality custom-published book,
drop by our website for more books and information.

www.winepresspublishing.com
"Your partner in custom publishing."